The Book of Emergencies

Second Edition

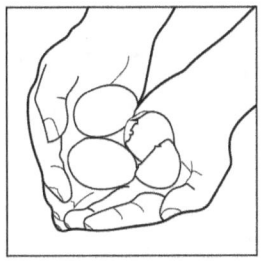

The Book of Emergencies

by Rosemarie Dombrowski

Second Edition

Five Oaks Press
FIVE-OAKS-PRESS.COM

Copyright © 2017 Rosemarie Dombrowski
All rights reserved. Second edition.

Five Oaks Press
Newburgh, NY 12550
five-oaks-press.com
editor@five-oaks-press.com

ISBN: 978-1-944355-42-5

Cover Art and Design: Lynn Marie Houston
Photo of the Author: Charissa Heckard

Printed in the United States of America

For B,
and all the mothers navigating these waters

CONTENTS

Preface: The Ethnography of Emergencies   1

I: Reconstruction
- The Grievance, the Wings   3
- Electrocution   5
- Provenience   6
- Reconstruction   7
- The Genetics of Love   8
- Sensory Perception   9
- Transference   11
- Flickerings   12
- Tableau   13
- Motor skills   14
- Milestone   15
- Chutes and Motors   16
- Case Study   17
- Tightrope   18
- Semantics   19

II: Erasure
- The Book of Emergencies   21
- Partial Prompting   22
- Condundrum   23
- Escape Artist   24
- Habituation   25
- Audiology   26
- Non-Identical Matching   27
- Etiology   28
- Decomposure   29
- Exodus   30
- Erasure   31
- Love/Intolerance   32
- Architecture of Despair   33

III: Revelation
        Subcutaneously 35
        Three Approximations of Maturity 36
        Relativity 37
        Spitting at the Moon 38
        The Trial 39
        The Verdict 40
        Revelation 41
        Parental Advisory 42
        Opus 43
        In the Event of an Emergency 44

Appendix A: 17 Reasons 47
Appendix A: 17 Letters 55

Acknowledgments 73

Autism is both a neurobiological disorder and a developmental disability. It can result in severe damage to neural pathways that control communication, social interaction, cognition, and motor skills; additionally, it can have a profound effect on physiological functions.

To date, no single cause or cure has been identified.

Preface: The Ethnography of Emergencies

The Book of Emergencies represents a personal-poetic attempt to capture the imagistic, linguistic, and emotional discombobulation of the world of autism. The poems exemplify moments of lucidity and love, perplexing exchanges, circuitous routes to nowhere (and somewhere), and the frustration that accompanies the cultural barrier between my world and my son's—the separation between the verbal and the non-verbal worlds.

In this way, the collection—in addition to being a love story—is like an ethnographic account of my fieldwork in another culture. It's the kind of story that only the colliding of two worlds could engender.

I often wonder if these poems are the only authentic record of the dizzying "middle years"—the years following the diagnosis of his congenital heart defects and the subsequent surgeries; the years following the autism diagnosis, the ones during which I threw myself headlong into the then-nascent community of biomedical researchers and the small coalition of doctors who were convinced that medical, therapeutic, and dietary interventions could reduce the severity of the mysterious disorder.

Those were the years when specialists ran obscure tests, attempted to decipher unpredictable results, then gave us even more obscure protocols to follow—protocols like a restricted rotation diet and a supplementation regimen; rigorous in-home habilitation, speech and occupational therapy, music and horseback riding therapy. Those were the years of interminable crying, daily meltdowns, frequent lashing out, and increasing self-injury. Those were the years in which we lived in a hermetically sealed world of treatments, and the improvements were slow to emerge.

But there's something to be said for agonizing persistence, how it can resurrect things that are lost, transform the abject into something bearable, even beautiful.

It's been over seventeen years since his birth—a birth that was also plagued by the diagnosis of a triad of life-threatening congenital heart defects—and almost fifteen since his autism diagnosis. In those years, he's only spoken a handful of decipherable words. He's grown warm and then cold and then warm again. There have been few constants in our relationship or our lives aside from these lyrical fieldnotes.

The impetus behind the appendices (17 Reasons and 17 Letters), composed in 2017, is similar. They catalogue the changed and the unchanged, observe the ongoing sorrows with new clarity, but the most significant departure is the direct addressee in the 17 Letters sequence. In other words, these poems are not about my son, but rather written to my son despite his inability to read or comprehend them. Maybe that's why they needed to be catalogued here, in the cultural archives of the readable world, and because inscription is my only form of communication.

Thus, the ongoing writing of the poems, like the protocols, has become a crucial means of imposing order and consistency on an otherwise chaotic world—a world that doesn't adhere to the rules of physics or language, a world that doesn't play by the rules of parent-child relations. They are a form of sustenance and survival, a search for the lyrical in the midst of an arduous investigative study. They continue to teach me how to speak a new language, and more importantly, how to occupy the space in between what is definitively *here* and what is questionably *there*—between the world we know, and the one we don't.

~ Rosemarie Dombrowski

I: Reconstruction

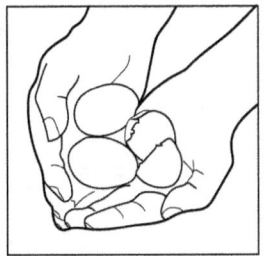

The Grievance, the Wings

He baptizes you with Digoxin
under panels of light.

Child of god, he says, *time is a construct
of the conscious mind.*

Someone walks by and closes the lid.
A woman is crying
on the other side of the island.

I sing riddles from Newbery's *Book of Rhymes,*
watch the blinking red light
that's whispering *life, the grievance,
the chain, the wings.*

Someone hands me a styrofoam cup
filled with coffee,
and I feel my stomach
beat against the current.

I lose track of time.
The machines are a metronome.

I write an address on the back of a card,
drive for miles in silence.
When I look at the card again,
the writing is unrecognizable.

Someone hands me a styrofoam cup
filled with coffee,
tells me that time is a construct,
life is suffering,
and therein lies the universe.

Electrocution

It begins in your hands, tiny hands
that dislocate their fingers like leaves,
veins crinkling silently to the ground.

You flip the switch to the *on* position,
awakening currents that escape
through your eyes and ears.

Yesterday, your thumb eclipsed the sun
like a frozen star, and you conducted the wind
with bamboo stalks throughout the afternoon.

Outside, it's raining like it was
the day that electricity was discovered.
The patterns in the clouds
are flocks of flying hands, the wisps of fingers
incandescent, then red,

debunking principles of physics.

Provenience

You are sacs of fluid surrounded by bone,
skin that whispers the secrets of breathing,
the pumping of ventricles laden with holes.

By afternoon, the windows are teeming
with jaundiced light, and the sill
is buzzing steadily with flies.

A paper bag sits on a portable tray.
Inside it, we discover a scrap of Gore-Tex
and a spool of thread,
a crudely drawn map
of the provenience of urgency.

Reconstruction

Your body has begun to harvest water,
so I cup my hand under your chin
like a saucer,
a medical reconstruction of anatomy,
a hole that signifies a lack of tissue or love.

All those hours,
I knew where to find you:
somewhere in the Midwest beside
birthday balloons and fishing line,
a magnifying glass used to read yellowing recipes.

With a sheet of instructions,
they patched your leaking vessel—
waves crashing like surgical sound,
your bloated body setting sail on the muddied river,
pointed toward home.

The Genetics of Love

Like you, I don't remember the one
who retrieved the rag,
began scrubbing the floor with Clorox
like a wearied janitor, grumbling
about the anatomy of boys.

When you bleed, you remove your shoes
like appendages, the ceramic shards
surrounding you like a dolmen,
the wind and the nearby cows
droning an ancient language.
Somewhere, someone is applying pressure
with butterfly wings, and the chambers of the heart
are pumping in quarter time.

After midnight, the towel is stained
with the history of silence,
and my hand is clutching bone,
balancing a synthetic tube
that connects us like roots. Together,
we inhale the contents of the bucket:

the uncertainty of sterile solution,
of anomalies,
of the genetics of love.

Sensory Perception

You are here and *not* here,
at the foot of the stairs in some
Victorian house that was never ours.

I say a benediction that resembles
a nursery rhyme about the moon.
The book is filled with poems and mittens,
a whispering chair that takes
the shape of purple flowers.

At dusk, I wash your feet
until the tub becomes a tiny garden—
miles of desert road,
the heavy weave of blankets
doused with hair,
the remnants of the horse's tumbleweeds.

The mirror is where we lose our teeth,
the meaning of our phonemes
hidden deep within the pipes beneath the sink.
Ten years from now, I'll retrieve them
like a linguist,
employ the science of translation,
the unearthing of corrosion-turned-song.

Beside the stove, you watch the color of your name
escape from my lips, the fractions
floating upwards from the searing beef.

In silence, the house is ours,
and you're breathing, belly-down,

inside the *here* that we've created—

here, where shapes are irregular,
and the color of equations is yet unsolved.

Transference

We practice the inexact science of healing,
the craft of equal parts agitation and heat,
the wrinkling of the dermis like time.

Behind the curtain of steam,
we succumb to the pitfalls of memory,
the memory of indifference,
the body's volume of water or loss.

As we sing, the alphabet morphs
into the table of elements.
Everything knowable is abbreviated and changed,
circling the drain.

When your body reappears, I note
the width of your torso, the bruised shin,
the lanky feet, all of which
you seem to have inherited from me.

Flickerings

I am here then there—

on a porch swing, late July,
a jar of fireflies beside me,
my mother's voice intruding
on the hiss-and-hum of the woods
behind our house.

Inside, the nightlight shines through the window
like a dying planet.

Back in your room, we call it a campfire,
your eyes bouncing off the flickering patterns,
the galaxy taking shape on the walls.

Tableau

Vowels circling like birds,
the sound of synapses chaotically mingling.

At the top of the hill,
thinking that the colors must be like stories.

You shriek with gusto at the design—
the streamers of sun on the grass,
this miniature of the world made
of impulse and blinding light.

Motor Skills

The doctor studies the rings around your eyes,
your proprioceptive capacity—
consecutive years of a poorly organized body
attempting to master airplane arms,
marching in time,
the tracking of a bird on a clear afternoon.

When you tongue the links of the fence,
you perceive the world for what it is—
solid, synthetic, perplexing.
You taste and smell your way
through the darkened house.

The textbook example states
that a person like you could never drive a car
due to his inability to *steer or use the foot pedals
while looking at the road ahead,*
and I agree.

Milestone

When your teeth went missing,
the shadows from the swing
spread out across the grass like a swell,
a contagion,
the disappearing act of childhood.

In the absence of molars,
you screwed your canines
into the counter,
marred the LPs with saliva
as you scavenged for food or sound.

You invert the principles of logic
as I chart the oddities by the hour,
the fading likelihood of progress.

Chutes and Motors

Your eyes become awkward,
fixated on the glare of sound
inside the car.
I drive for miles without considering
the signs that you're obsessively counting,
the number of stoplights
between *there* and *home*.

Somewhere inside, messages are lost
to closure and time, a slightly irregular,
delicate path of existence.

At the post office, you hear the idling
of imagination in the foreground.
Everything you know (or never will)
is sealed inside,
slid down the darkened chute
that holds your secrets.

Case Study

You are his, you are ours,
you are something indefinable
in the space between normalcy and catastrophe.

Today, I pruned the unplanted trees
down the street,
the yard where I envision you humming.
Your body is burdened, older,
and I imagine them asking, me conceding,
you living vacantly behind glass,
electrodes like vines sprouting
from your scalp, saucer-shaped rings
and a host of unknown parasites.

In the absence of natural light,
you become foreign, less knowable than before,
and I follow suit.

Tightrope

Even the arches of recycled water
couldn't stop you—
your cumbersome feet
slamming into chrome parts,
everything struggling to master the
dynamics of sight and space.

When your palms begin to sweat,
you cling to my forearm and thigh,
reminiscent of some love
that we thought we'd forgotten.
You scream and I mimic the sound,
inserting your name into the weighty atmosphere.

When you crane your head to find me,
I weave a net with my eyes.
I pause to consider the magic of tightrope walkers,
who, like you, speak another language.

Semantics

Your speech began yesterday,
contextually out of sorts
and with faulty intonation.

At 3:05, themes recurred like holes—
a walnut-shaped heart, a shard of
damaged bone, the repetition of self
and sound to nowhere.

By 4:15, your fidgeting limbs
attempted a rough translation, your words
reduced to figment denotations.

By evening, I sense the meaning of spaces,
what I find between the hard *c* and the
viscous *y*. I end my words with lulling sounds,
patterns of green and gentle rocking.

You, I say, *you.*

II: Erasure

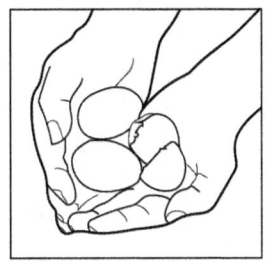

The Book of Emergencies

Wordlessness, then the shame of your sounds—
indefinite, infinite humming
absorbed into nibbled edges of paper,
pages containing an elephant, a tiger,
a mother and son hedgehog eating lunch.

I open the book of emergencies to page sixty-four,
randomly peruse the croup, tinnitus,
myopia in the park.
As I read, the words become cells
that bounce between organs:
the uselessness of flagella,
the conundrum of electrons loosed from their orbit.
Even the index is scrambled,
droning the names that we know by heart,
the diagnostics of the obvious, speak-able world.

After hours of research, I mix a concoction,
inject, start over again.
And you continue to hum.

Partial Prompting

First *block*, then *crayon*, then *ball*—
the afternoon, table-top rotation
resembling a cheap magician's trick.

Before exasperation,
I recognize the shape of futility in the room,
the methodical heart-beat of indifference that
pulses through your veins.
For years, I've ignored your hatred of nouns,
your love of the verbs that define your existence:
eat, sleep, watch, repeat.

In some way, we've all been deceived—

you preferring the streamers of light
that trail behind your fingertips,
me preferring the sound of consonants,
analytical phrases scrawled into margins,
the way beauty becomes a polluted concoction
of what it never should have been,
what none of us ever imagined.

Conundrum

You are the failure of moveable parts,
a wreck of morphology and function,
a study in misdirected gaits.

For you, I degrade the language,
tell you to *sit* then *open,*
fork the remains of the plate into your mouth
like a biological experiment,
like the replication of some Darwinian feat—
a debacle of nurturing,
a series of modifications gone awry.

I linger in your odorous skin.
I pray for the relief of conundrums.

By sunset, you've mastered the confusion
of light and sound, and you're gazing toward apathy
as though it's a direction.

Escape Artist

> *For want of a nail the shoe was lost...*
> —ancient proverb

Under cover of rain you escape us,
drawn by the incongruence of rock,
its rolling motion under the balls of your feet,
the slim chance of edibility.

Unnoticed, you arrive at the corner,
pause in the absence of signifiers—
the security of replications and rhyming verses,
the hubris of well-crafted phrases
you'll never comprehend.

When we retrieve you, I whisper
sounds of desperation into your ear,
beg you to stay a little while longer.

Habituation

Despite the fragile state in which I find you—
afflicted and mute, confused
by your worldly surroundings—
there's something less pathetic
about the mid-week pitch of your cry.

Like most things I've loved
or made habitual,
I know this by heart—
begin with essential washing,
persist in the evening liturgy,
continually pray for equilibrium,
the capacity to remain steady,
to grasp a fork with one hand.

Audiology

The window has crippled us,
and the carpet reeks of secret names,
embedded like stains.

I dream of a long ride to Mexico,
the mind's ability to heal
or drown itself in gulf-stream waters.

Here, we practice the act of ascension,
marking the world in decibels of light:
tympani to the left,
acoustic reflex on the right.
Within an hour, you will forget
the shape of sound.
I will praise your attempts
in lieu of meaningful conversation.
Like you, I am rote and unforgiving,
forgetful and slow to process.

The days earn us nothing.
You writhe on my lap
until they're convinced of your
near-perfect hearing.

Non-Identical Matching

Standing beside the overturned carton of milk,
you study the pattern of pooling liquid,
oblivious to the *hand-over-hand* method
by which we sop, wring, repeat
until the tile reappears.

Like anyone, I expected to recite them from memory—
matrilineal nursery rhymes,
an anthology of blues—
singing in unison while our arms
drafted a radical scale of syncopation,
the lilting sounds of the sea and
an assemblage of farm animals
surrounding the wails of a plastic horn,
the gypsy-oddity of a blue and white tambourine.

In the aftermath of milk and nostalgia,
I study the theory of mercurial burdens,
your blood coursing through the annals of medical science:

the science of misanthropic concerns,
the dread of the neuro-typical population,
their eventual extinction by the likes of you.

Etiology

When the milk expired,
we knew nothing of starvation,
of the fish that live for years in the Pacific,
barely evading the nets of immigrants,
bloated with drugs and tin.

Like a virus or toxin, the ocean lies
its way into your cells, guileless and sacred.
We scrutinize organisms,
insert ink diagrams into your file,
bulging with numbers and unreal solutions.

But nothing is ever what it seems,
and now, even science can't save you.

Decomposure

When the window shattered, you were
just below the horizon,
the sky congesting with engines and lights
that we always mistook for stars.

When they disappear, I wonder at the difference
between *loss* and *lost*, *fading* and *finality*,
the ways in which language can't suffice
or refuses to show itself.

Last night, I confused you with the others—
verbally sophisticated, anatomically defined.

Today, you are indisputable proof of the worst of
our theories—
all frailty and decay,
less complicated by muscle and hair,
speaking in tongues to desperate, haunted women.

Exodus

For months you've looked at photographs,
attempted to choose the one that corresponds
to the name that's being spoken.

Utterance one: nonsense.
Utterance two: syllabic sound.
Utterance three: the language
you don't speak becomes discernible,
the words morphing into purposeful cognates,
related by letters and blood.

Your father has left the country,
and I find myself repeating
the word *gone* like a mantra.
I've noticed that when I say it three times,
it sounds like finality.

Erasure

There are no more defenses against
corruption or pollutants,
no land masses unburdened by spills
or the sound of bulldozers
rising out of dusty, ancient graves.

You vacuum your hippocampus
while I tend to the floors,
attempt to rid the air of particulates
and bacteria.
Your memory must be
the only renewable resource for miles.

Today, I will wipe your mouth
with an unbleached napkin,
reminding myself of the virtue of recycling,
the compassion of sustainable acts.

Tonight, I will better understand
the likelihood of erasure,
the risk of chaining yourself to a tree
or a fence or a doorjamb,
the fantasy of leaping off the roof
with you clutched in my arms.

Love/Intolerance

I discover you crouched
in a damp corner of bedding,
envelop you in my arms like the tiny swallow
that was birthed on the rafter.
For weeks I've prepared tea
to a concert of infantile shrieking,
secretly wishing it dead.

The line between love and intolerance
is not an equation.
In the absence of quotients,
hours assume odors and sounds:
4:15, the cleanness of silence,
6:45, the raucous of searing meat.
Our minds shift like the time,
dictated by smell, my repulsion
absolved (and renewed) by the hour.

Tomorrow, there will only be you,
morphing between low notes and rancorous fumes.
And the swallow will have flown away.

The Architecture of Despair

Driving through gunfire,
the risk of a wrought-iron fence,
an open canal that flows toward the mouth of alfalfa.
Near the ramshackle house, the boys
keep vigil under the trees,
screwing Parliament filters into the clay
that holds the neighborhood together.

When I ask you to build me a city,
you find yourself miles from Broadway,
lost under arches of color and love,
a bucket of symmetrical, plastic pieces.

Driving, I imagine you next to me,
imagining nothing,
my elbow chafed by the nearby despair,
imagining worse things than this silence.

III: Revelation

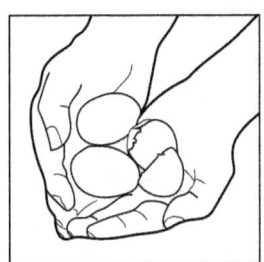

Subcutaneously

The nurses restrain you.
Like the others,
you bleed before the bandage
adheres to your dampened skin.

In the office, the body is reduced to diagrams,
black and white chains and
the breakdown of proteins.
You watch the birds in periphery,
disrobe in the playroom
to the sound of rustling papers:
yellow for arsenic, red for copper.

Once, someone told me that
the skin is our largest organ, the most
viable escape route for toxins and waste.
When you dive beneath it, gently,
you discover a layer of tissue that
insulates the body,
absorbs trauma, provides energy.

Inside, the cells multiply and die,
becoming more normal by the hour.
As they move—intuitively, beautifully—
wounds are miraculously healed.

Three Approximations of Maturity

1.

Your fingers were stained with red dye #5.

I wiped them after every bite,
oblivious to encroaching adolescence,
your ability to make your way
back to the row of cars
and know which one was ours.

2.

The sky was the color of salmon,
and the car was a silvery-blue.

My hand buttressed your torso
as we veered to avoid it,
the stability of rubber wheels
propelling us forward.

3.

I realize you've known this all along—
that faith gave birth to science
inside temples of equations.

I ponder the laws of physics
as you try to touch the sky
on rusted chains.

Relativity

You are beautiful now,
fleetingly docile,
nearer to perfection
than anything I've almost created.

You are older than I imagined,
living in a dream
in which no one speaks the language
that's almost translatable.

For years I've observed you,
written you like a memory
because I know the story of loss,
how little an image can do
to resurrect that which has passed.

Spitting at the Moon

There's a break between word and image,
a pause after *whispering hush.*

As I wipe your chin, you gaze at the ceiling,
the wonderment of a thousand constellations,
the low-glow of a celestial halo
on a field of muted blue.

Last year, there were planets circling the sky,
and you would spit at the moon as it tangled
around earth's fishing-line-string,
knocked the ring off of Saturn
and split Neptune in two.

The stars would scatter across the floor
like embers, their clear, sharp edges
sticking to our toes,
injuring the harmony between spaces,
the telescopic beauty of impossible distances.

The Trial

In Hawthorne, the child is mute, oddly
disempowered
yet a breeder of unease.

Some interpret this as possession,
which is exactly what the the historians
would have us believe.

The Verdict

You, on the other hand,
are likely of both worlds,
fueled by intolerable heat and
decadent tufts of light,

something defective
yet strangely nearer to perfection.

Revelation

Soon, someone will reveal the errors in calculation,
the act of synthesis gone terribly wrong.

I pause on *error*, repeating the word
to the walls, the cold cinder,
the non-perishables in the pantry that could
sustain us for days in our snow-bound,
sub-zero delirium.

When your skin becomes distressed,
we retreat to the basement,
find a clean, white sheet,
silently count the beams above our heads.
The bulb swings like a pendulum,
like the ominous warning that it is.

Nothing lasts forever:
not electricity, not the body,
not the bond between a doe and her young.

When the drifts subside, we pry open the door,
watch the last flutter of a bird's wing rolling leeward,
forced by wind and other unseen elements.

Parental Advisory

I watch as you disappear over the edge
of a landscape painting,
morph into a tale about a boy
tumbling into an invisible garden.

Despite the density of silence, I manage to find you—
motionless, face-down in the ravine.
I discover what it means to be inconsolable,
wail like a woman in Gaza, Haiti, Sudan,
some forsaken place
where language has lost its purpose.

You are my dog in the night wandering,
barking lunacy into the morning,
bitter stench of urine rollicking beneath the sheets.

When I reach for you, my arm disappears,
my mind overtaken by the
void where they've placed you—
your body splitting open, pouring forth
its contents into some other vessel,
one more fit for navigating imaginary terrain.

Opus

After this, what's left for us to write?

Maybe the perfect melancholy of silence,
the way it fills your ears with suspicion,
medicinal drownings in the Phoenix dusk.

Write me a sonata in at least three movements,
laden with academics and adagio.
Make it uneven, in a key of flat,
plagued by ringing and synapse,
the musical lament of disease.

For you, I've written this story of beautiful madness:
what it slows, what it makes possible
without sense or translation.

The keys are the key,
and some are always missing—
the ones in the drawer
unlocking nothing that we need.

In the Event of an Emergency

The afternoon festers like a wound,
and I realize that this is everything
I've never liked about the body.
You trouble me like that—
like repulsion or an elusive cure,
like the hoax-remedies of pagan healers:
ambrosial meat and moldy apples,
rank fish and rotten berry.

I lean against the counter
and lick juice from the crevices,
watch it pool on the granite beneath my elbows.
I listen to Mariachi music, sleep sporadically
and shower at odd times of the night.
I ignore the reports sent home
by the school psychologist.

I'm falling in love with someone else's identity
because faith is a myth, an unsustainable story,
hack-science that's been FedExed across the Atlantic
in the middle of the mountain-standard night.

I refuse to open the envelopes that contain the results.
Instead, I write messages in the spaces
between *recipient* and *sender*,
things like *the narrative of self-defeat is cyclical,*

commonly exaggerated, oftentimes untrue.

*And it's not really an emergency
unless we choose to see it as one.*

Appendix A: 17 Reasons

for B, Naoki Higashida, and all the boys afflicted with nonverbal autism

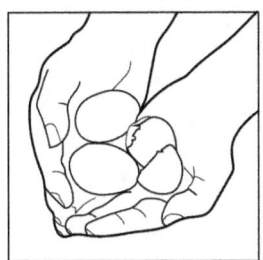

a sentence is a non-verbal grid of symbols

I've forgotten where I left off, why I stopped
believing in the art of programming pictures onto a screen,
when I grew tired of digitized voices.

But I still want to know what's hammering away at your head
—the exquisite corpse of your dreams, the surrealistic
language that's locked inside you.

against the status quo

This is a story about un-remembering, about hearing and not
listening, like what your grandmother used
to call *in one ear and out the other.* She didn't
realize that there was an entire species of you, interpreting
oceanic sounds without seashells,
ebbing and flowing with the tide.

Still, we persist in the experiment, white-knuckling ourselves
into the hundredth repetition as the waves carry you away
into oblivion.

(in)sensitivity

It's like a disease that protects you from the
etiology of despair. Your nerves, like your
memories, are jumbled. I never trim your hair, and your
nails are clipped to ruination.

I try to imagine what you see: a puzzle missing 17 pieces.

I try to imagine what remains: the directions for taking a shower, the motor planning required to steer your bicycle away from the canal.

oddities of sound

It's the not knowing how, the holding back that's painful—like self-strangulation, like when you wrap your forearm around my neck and tighten it like a vice.

Your decibels are not genetic. Your voice is like a breath, familiar and reflexive, but it's not for me to hear.

the water outside of time

The primordial ooze, the Cambrian freedom, the single-celled beauty of the *pulse of time*.

You are outside the world, inside a dream where everything is edible, where the body isn't hurtling through space, pulling against your current.

This is the opposite of a mystery.

un-remembering

You forget quickly or never remember. I continue
to repeat the questions because the rhythm of the words is a sound that we arrange for the sake of
play rather than conversation.

But memory isn't a linear path that you can chart with a string, like a cartographer tracing the routes of interstates.

Memory is a series of dots, some of which are outliers that will never be connected.

the echo in the room

You're fishing for clues, evading capture by the nets of predators like me.

You shuffle through the deck until the picture matches the sound that you're repeating like a refrain.

But feelings aren't patterns, and there's no answer key to rely on, and you'll never understand why I'm crying.

intonation is a language

The words you're not saying are the only ones flying from your mouth, dancing across the screen that you've fashioned out of molecules of air.

Likewise, the story is always missing because the words are untranslatable, a maddening cycle of variable intonations.

And the words that you're almost using are predictably similar in shape and size, rectangular like a block, unable to fit through conventional door or windows.

aloneness is a state of being

When I lean in to touch you, I think about indifference to time or a broken windchime, the torn pages littering the floor like a snowstorm.

Nothing is ever perfect with you, but when I think about it, nothing is ever perfect without you.

eyes and ears (and mouth and nose)

The eyes are not the windows to anything, but the voices are seeable, touchable things. You reach for the hibiscus past midnight, moan agreeably at the illuminated dust, sniff at the passing cars.

It's not about holding on or letting go. It's the glow of the world that distracts you.

lost and found

There's no fear in wandering, in the act of endless movement over infinite streets made of aimless existence. No beginning and no end. No sense of loss until you feel it, acutely, the loss of something tangible, maybe a shoe, and the skin on your sole begins to peel away like plastic, like something that's about to disintegrate, transform from a solid to a liquid to a gas, invisible to everyone, including yourself.

(un)freedom

Freedom is an ironic state of being when the only things you understand are the things you already understand.

I think about Franklin, the auto-didacts of history, the self-educated women of the 18th century. How I descended from them. How you descended from me. How unable I am to teach you the art of motivation.

the worst things may not be the worst

You are the problem-causers, the instigators of disaster, the perpetual catastrophes-in-waiting.

When you hear this, you retreat to a corner and lament your human form.

A hardship is defined as *severe suffering or privation.* A form of *destitution, poverty, [and] penury, adversity [and] pain.*

I wonder how severe any of this really is: the twisted cords, the chewed curtains, the sheets smelling of urine for days.

goodbye to you/me

There won't be dancing, at least not in the conventional sense. The martial arts will always be impossible. Your imitation dilemmas have been well-documented through the ages.

It's possible, however, that you are the most evolved of the species, unconsciously reflexive, unable to delineate between self and other in your head, heart, or hand.

You are, perhaps, a genetic error of remarkable proportions. On the other hand, you could be signaling the collapse of the divides that will destroy us.

anti-linear behavior

You are the bike path that loops around the canal. You are videos on perennial repeat.

Your brain is an electrical storm, intermittently explosive and prone to thunderous sounds in the night.

I spent years denying these things, but the studies don't lie.

You compulsively shred paper. I compulsively bite my lip. We share multiple axes in the diagnostic manual. We are disordered and disabled. We are the silent confusion of acronyms: ASD, OCD, BDD, ICD, BFRB, SMD.

the body issue

It wants to be invisible like thoughts, like the fear of thoughts becoming visible tangible things.
Like sweatpants in the summer.

It wants socks with no clothing, shirts without tags. It wants to be untouched. It wants to control that which it cannot control; at the very least, to not be controlled by the touches of others.

Your body is the desert after a monsoon rain, slightly pungent and sweet. You want to feel your skin come alive, so you open the window, and you absorb one another, singing like sponges that have reached their point of saturation.

the innocence of plot

It's simple to follow, like a series of childhood clues, like a trail of breadcrumbs. It's the gentle sound of birds singing familiar songs in far-away places. It's an antiquated nursery rhyme filled with repetition, the cadence carrying you away into rooms without walls, streets lined with trees and plants and green, what you might refer to as the color of being alive.

Appendix B: 17 Letters

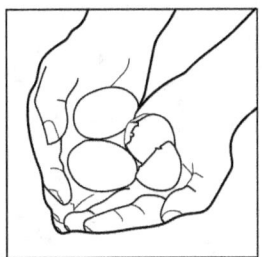

Dear B,

I'm going to speak with a bird in my mouth
because the words will be less significant than the gestures.
You've taught me that this is often the case.

We're hiking a trail for the first time.
It's almost sunset, and the orange haze
is approaching the mountains like an embrace.
You shirk from it momentarily, like touch.

We see a family from India, and the youngest
cranes his neck to watch you ascend.
His mother redirects his gaze.
I repeatedly ask you to watch where you're going
but I realize that when you don't know
where you are in the first place, it's an impossible request.

I say the words *rock* and *tree* because I know
the value of linguistic simplicity.
I know which battles will cost us the war.
I can predict the outcome of almost any scenario because
you've forced me to master the art of clairvoyance.

Once, I saw us floating down a river,
your body slackened and still,
and I knew you were returning to the source—
Cambrian, womb, or otherwise.

I realize that resistance is futile,
that prophets are often draped in disguises,
their messages drowned in a paradigm
that never applied to us, and never will.

Dear B,

These things on my dress are called polka dots.
I know that you will never understand nuance,
like the difference between violet and plum.

What I'm seeing out the window is called a peak.
To my right, the Santa Catalinas.
These things you call trucks are captains of industry.
Acceleration is the force by which
we defy the natural order of physics.

The cat's eye is literally a cat's eye,
but it also has something to do with marbles and dice,
the reflectors that separate lanes on the freeway.

In the hour before sunset, they say
that the sun's UV rays are less dangerous,
but the only thing you need to remember
is that everything requires protection from something.

Dear B,

Four hours I've listened to the water
splashing around the screen of your device.
When the battery dies, you'll use pools of saliva
to recreate the effect.
It's impossible to deny your intuitive talents.

You are surrounded by extremes and always have been,
but there's no need for apologies.
You are a product of Libra rising,
of genetic amalgamations
that will go unexplained for centuries.
We are the age of Aquarius in both pitch and song.

When I ask you to dance, you tell me how to move
with your eyes. When we change direction,
I watch you struggle to re-orient your limbs.
You have never been rhythmical,
but your interpretive arms have enveloped city blocks,
mesmerized strangers like a murmuration of birds.

We live in a universe of perpetual firsts,
of inaugural washings and dryings.
And every time I hold you, it's like we're beginning.

Dear B,

I never leave the house without offering prayers to the sun.
I may have been a priest in the life before this one.

A prayer is a supplication or statement of praise.
Sometimes, it transports you into a state of meditation.

Imagine that you're high and you close your eyes,
and you see your lives appearing in different patterns,
the geography of place represented in synapse of color.
And when the patterns disappear
you are a country in transit, an extravagant learner
moving in the opposite direction of time,
and so you allow yourself to become
a native in a new land, a student of the minutia,
of the beauty that flashes
through the eye of your gut, blooming with ideas.

And you will know you have arrived
when you begin crafting letters with your hands,
when the smallest units of meaning are the ones
that you stow away for the journey.

Dear B,

I'm still waiting for you to tell me if you were
dreaming of loneliness or the sound of a waterfall,
the hands of a compassionate man
massaging your quarter-sized heart
or the arms of an unknown nurse enveloping you.

I've told you that there was frost on the window that day,
that every window is a portal,
that everything visible is moving
beneath a layer of Sonoran ice in another dimension.

I'm telling you now that there was something celestial
in the numbers that hovered above you,
something other-worldly in your blackened eyes,
like the mysteries of Mary and gestation,
the psychic line of Magdalene
that tore its way through the fragile membrane,
leaving a hole that I could stuff
with murmurs and groans, seed pods and wind,
all sorts of unquantifiable things.

Dear B,

There is no way to explain the interpersonal ruins
under which you are trapped,
your leg un-tickled for weeks,
your friend disappeared into the Paleocene.

But I can assure you that continents are taking shape,
that he has been rebirthed as an ape or a whale,
maybe even a horse.
If he resides at the top of the food chain,
he is an enormous bird.

I think all of these things would please you,
but it still doesn't explain why no one has
pumped the bicycle tires
or instructed you to stop at the crossing.
It doesn't explain where the banjo has gone,
or why the van has driven away.

Summer is approaching, and I will refuse
to light the oven for months.
There will be no more cake.
We will honor the moratorium,
suffering together while singing the same old songs,
slightly off key and without any harmonies.

Dear B,

It's futile to tell you this, but you need to know
that a poem consisting of one sentence is like a baby
born with as many limbs as a goddess in India,
limbs that the parents refuse to amputate
for spiritual reasons, which is the antithesis of the disorder
that leads someone to believe that one or more of their limbs
are extraneous, useless to their body, counter to their being,
like words are to you, like the pronunciation keys
that your grandmother used to dole out like candy when I
    was four,
workbooks filled with recycled-gray pages that spoke of rules
I wasn't supposed to learn until first or second grade,
which reminds me of little Dominic,
your pre-school classmate who used to walk
the perimeter of the fence every day,
tapping his ear and screaming gently into the distance—
this was something that you weren't supposed to learn
until many years later, or not at all.

Dear B,

Please forgive me for revealing these stories,
for inscribing them like an interviewer, an interloper,
an anthropologist in the field of our kitchen
or the exotic space of your bedroom.

I feel obligated to record these sessions.
There are people who need to understand
that we are older now, more content,
half-toilet trained and able to rinse our own dishes.
We are less physically prompted,
more intuitively able to follow the steps
required of us to take showers,
better able to navigate sidewalk and street.

Sometimes, we still cry at coffeeshops,
disappear into the dirt-filled crevice between window
    and table,
a place where a lame bird might go to nurse its wing.

We are surgical reconstructions of imperfection.
Little has come to us naturally,
though we have learned that the cycles of the heart
begin in the right ventricle,
sporadically emit tenderness
and return through the left atrium,
escape through the aorta into the congenital body,
the biological systems that will never know empathy,
the ones that are unable to be nurtured back to life.

Dear B,

I want you to know that the bipolarity of the heart
is directly related to the seasons.

Someone may tell you that he likes to drink coffee
under a layer of stratus clouds,
but what inevitably follows is an altostratus of the mind,
a glassy haze over the eyes,
a phenomenon that turns birdsong to silence,
the delicate branches of a jacaranda
into nooses of dangling nests.

But after a thunderstorm, the negative ions
purify the air, removing pollutants and pathogens.
And the pounding surf is a powerful antidepressant.
I remember the waterfalls in Supai and Oahu,
how I'd never felt more content.

Dear B,

We've hiked the trail four times now,
always on Sunday, possibly because
that's what feels familiar—
the act of worshipping something
at a designated time and place,
the transcendentalism of the desert in bloom,
the not fully knowing the power of anything
despite the science that explains
photosynthesis and geologic time.

I'm starting to think I might be a Jew,
which is difficult to explain
outside my belief in the miraculous resilience
of a long line, a floating love poem,
or waterlilies catching on fire.

Despite what everyone says,
I'm not sure how far I've come.
For instance, I'm still questioning the meaning of signs,
obsessively photographing dead birds.
The last one was lying on its belly,
its mauve neck twisted gently to the right.
Its eyes were closed, and I think there were
a few drops of blood next to its beak.
I think I was meant to see this,
to notice the details.

Still, I'm not sure what that makes me.

Dear B,

Your father has left more times than I can count.
You don't know what currency is,
so I don't bother telling you
that he's been a good provider
(which is something men like to hear).

In truth, *I* am the good provider.

I've scrubbed and repainted the stained walls,
refilled the syringes with cardiac meds
and mail-order supplements,
driven you home in lieu of abandonment.

I've detangled your dreadlocked hair,
trimmed your mustache with tiny scissors,
helped you wash yourself through every stage of puberty.

You have needed me more times than I can count.
You have taught me that love isn't a solvable equation.

Dear B,

I want to say something about durability,
endurance, what you've taught me
about these seemingly impossible concepts.

Nearly everyone was dead by the time I was fourteen.
Only your grandmother and I survived
the Midwestern years.

I have never known how to love a man and keep him,
and by keep him I mean keep him safe,
treat him tenderly, nurture him,
watch him grow slowly, over time, like a plant,
like the ones I tended during the promiscuous years,
the ones that taught me the sturdiness of the rubber tree,
the reliability of the philodendron and the bromeliad,
what it means to be constant, consistent, perennial,
to lose something and regrow it,
to resurrect yourself from a clod of dirt.

I have tended to some things well,
like the study of words and plants,
things that couldn't talk back.

Ironically, things like you.

Dear B,

There are times when I measure the weeks
by the number of broken capillaries on my legs,
the hours by the pressure needed to stop
the bleeding in my mouth and ears.

There are times when I eat for the sake of silence,
because the act of swallowing verbs and interrogatives
is less painful than the loop of *I-hate-yous*
and the *What-the-fuck-is-wrong-with-yous?*

I've stopped saying grace because I fear the power of words.
In truth, I stopped saying grace years ago.

Instead, I've begun storing up my gratitude
for the days in which you button your shirt,
sweep the crumbs without incident or bloodshed,
produce only sounds that signify or feign forgiveness.

Dear B,

I've complained too long,
lamented the disabled body
and its inability to hike South Mountain
or do a forward fold.

But your short-term memory is free of these toxins,
like our food and detergent, the small batches
of deodorant that I mix on the weekends,
and for this I should be grateful.

Instead, I spend hours obsessing over cotton sheets,
soap with less than four ingredients,
toothpaste that you can swallow by the teaspoon.
Sometimes, the act of over-doing
is a form of penance for all the things we've un-done,
all the apathy-turned-frustration,
the muteness replaced by theatrical meltdowns
and pulsing blue veins,
the thin skin that covers the heart
that will eventually destroy me.

Dear B,

A few weeks ago, I began using the term
higher self in casual conversation, as though
the canonical knowledge of the Buddhists and Jews
had been transmitted to me
in the space of a long-form poem,
an angelic, eight-part dream.

I'm not sure which was the case.

There are no photographs,
no smudges or orbs to analyze,
no halos behind the heads of the high-sighted or the dead.

I'm relieved that you can't have a crisis of consciousness,
that you've been unable to adopt a system of belief,
that you are, instead, an esoteric pagan
speaking in tongues to wolves and creosote,
dry riverbeds and the light of the harvest moon.

There's little else worth understanding here—
in the desert, the heart, or elsewhere.

Dear B,

You have chewed through the shower curtain like a rat,
like a character in a dystopian novel
searching for an unwrapped gem
amidst the trash of humanity.

The seal between tub and tile is broken,
expanding under the weight of arsenic-laden water.
When the room reaches capacity,
you will stand in the hall and say nothing.

But what you don't understand is that
I'm not a life raft,
not even a block of unmolded cheese
or an undented can of corn.

Everything is brimming toward apocalypse.
If only you could see that the streets are filled with it,
that our minds, like the tub,
are overflowing with its poisons.

Dear B,

Your heart has always been a cave in the forest,
the hollow of an old Midwestern tree
weakened by disease,
scaffolded by make-shift tourniquets and rituals.

Under the lights in the exam room,
I count the hairs on your chin.
The number 39 seems both big and small.
We are distracted by the antics of an anthropomorphic cat.
Like the fish, I'm expected to be the voice of reason.

I realize that the house will be destroyed
regardless of the intubation machine
or the one that translates cardiac rhythms.
Magic is, after all, just another means of postponing
    acceptance.

Instead, we become more rational,
teach ourselves to measure fractions
in the absence of hope:
subtract 61 from the left ventricle,
eject the mitral valve and cord,
place the cuff on your right index finger
as I clench your left hand,
rubbing my lips across your knuckles
while reciting the lines
I will not let you fall,
I will hold you up high
As I stand on a ball,
brush the stray curls from your eyes
as the percentages catapult to the floor,

continue murmuring the same phrases I have for years, not quite believing any of them.

ACKNOWLEDGMENTS

"Non-Identical Matching" appeared in *Tipton Poetry Journal*, Spring 2008.

The Book of Emergencies #2 & #7 ("The Genetics of Love" & "Tightrope") appeared in *Salt River Review*'s 10th Anniversary Issue, Spring 2008.

"Revelation Winter" appeared in *Phoenix Poetry Series Retrospective*, September 2011.

Poems 1, 5, 7, 8, and 10 from *17 Letters* appeared in *Birds Piled Loosely* (BPL), October 2017.

17 Letters appeared in the South Carolina Writer's Association annual publication, *The Petigru Review*, in October of 2017. The sequence, which appeared as prose, was also the recipient of the Carrie McCray Memorial Literary Award in Nonfiction.

www.ingramcontent.com/pod-product-compliance
Lightning Source LLC
Chambersburg PA
CBHW071747080526
44588CB00013B/2179